GERMAN SUPERCARS
PORSCHE • AUDI • MERCEDES

Paul Mason

W

FRANKLIN WATTS

LONDON•SYDNEY

Franklin Watts
First published in Great Britain in 2017 by
The Watts Publishing Group

Executive editor: Adrian Cole
Series designer: Mayer Media
Design manager: Peter Scoulding
Picture researcher: Diana Morris

Photo acknowledgements:
Abstract/Shutterstock: 10b. AnabelA88/
Shutterstock: 7b, 9t, 19tr, 21bl, 25b.
Apollo Arrow: 6-7, 7t. Artzz/Dreamstime:
3b, 30br. Audi: 1t, 3c,8c, 8-9, 10-11, 11b.
Pieter B/autogesport: 29cl. Bayerische
Motoren Werke AG: 1b, 5t, 12-13, 13t,
14-15, 15t. Ermess/Shutterstock: 30cl.
Matthew Gaussage/Alamy: 4-5. LOTEC :
28t. Mercedes-Benz: 16-17, 17t, 18t, 18-19,
28c, 29b, 31. Sam Moores/Shutterstock:
front cover t. Porsche A.G: 3t, 20-21. 21br,
22-23, 23t, 24-25, 24b, 26t, 26-27, 29t,
32. Alexandre Prévot Photographie: 28b.
Darin Schnarbel © 2012. Courtesy of RM
Auctions: 29cr. Superstock: 4t. Jordan Tan/
Dreamstime: 30tl. Denis Van der Water/
Dreamstime: 30tr. Miro Vrlilk Photography/
Shutterstock: front cover b. Wikimedia
Commons: 30b.

ISBN 978 1 4451 5097 0

Printed in China

Franklin Watts
An imprint of
Hachette Children's Group
Part of The Watts Publishing Group
Carmelite House
50 Victoria Embankment
London EC4Y 0DZ

An Hachette UK Company
www.hachette.co.uk

www.franklinwatts.co.uk

MIX
Paper from
responsible sources
FSC® C104740

FSC
www.fsc.org

Words highlighted in **bold** can
be found in the glossary

In 1885, a German engineer called Karl Benz made a vehicle called a *Motorwagen*. It had three wheels, seats like a horse-drawn carriage ... and a petrol engine. It was the first petrol-powered car.

OK, it doesn't look much like a supercar, but this 1885 Benz Motorwagen *was the start of the story of the car.*

SUPERCAR MANUFACTURERS

Karl Benz's company would one day become Mercedes Benz, which now makes some of the world's greatest supercars. They are not the only supercar makers in Germany, though. Audi and BMW also build cutting-edge supercars. So do specialist firms such as Apollo and 9ff. But the most famous German supercar maker is Porsche. Porsche has been making high-performance cars ever since it released the first 911 model, in 1964.

Engine: most supercars have **mid-mounted** engines, but the 911's engine is rear mounted

Price Tag...

The first 911s cost the equivalent of about £4,500. Today, a 1964 Porsche 911 would cost you over £150,000 – possibly a lot more, depending on what condition the car is in. That's almost double the price of a brand-new 911 Carrera!

Engine layout: the 911 has a **flat-6** engine, which is unusual: most supercars have a V-shaped engine layout

Seating: the 911 is a **2+2**: it has two front seats, and two small seats in the back. This makes the 911 one of only a few supercars with room for more than one passenger!

Drive: like many supercars, the 911 has rear-wheel **drive**

The BMW 503 (1954) **convertible** was made in limited numbers, largely because production costs over ran.

JUST WHAT *IS* A SUPERCAR?

There is no agreed definition of what makes a car a supercar. It could be some or all of these things:

- really expensive
- made in tiny numbers
- as high-performance as possible
- very fast, and probably very light
- tricky to drive
- useless for bringing home a week's shopping, going on a camping trip, taking kids to school, etc.

Even though it was designed over half a century ago, the first Porsche 911 shares many features with today's version.

Body shape: although it looks different from a modern 911, if you park the two side-by-side you can see they are related

200 kph
(125 mph)

0–100 KPH
9.1 seconds

MAX POWER
96 kw
(129 bhp) @ 6,100 rpm

MAX **TORQUE**
174 Nm
(128lb/ft) @ 4,600 rpm

 Max RPM:
6,100

 Engine:
1991 cc flat-6

 Weight:
1,080 kg

 Fuel use per 100 km (estimated):
21 litres

 CO2:
not known

 Gearbox:
5-speed

 Drive:
rear wheels

 Main body:
steel

 Frame:
steel

Braking:
hydraulic discs

ARROW

The name alone is enough to make you want to see an Arrow. And if you ever see one howl past at 360 kph, you will understand where they got the name. This car flies! The Arrow was designed by Roland Gumpert as a race-ready, but street legal, car.

The Arrow's styling is inspired by sharks. Not only a shark's streamlined shape and speed through the water – but also its aggressive, attacking nature. When the car starts, its engine snaps and snarls as the driver pushes the accelerator. The sound of the burbling exhausts is loud even when the Arrow isn't moving. The roar as the Arrow pulls away is deafening! Not for long, though – the Arrow can hit 200 kph in 8.8 seconds.

The Arrow was developed from one of the world's fastest cars, the Gumpert Apollo. In 2009 the Gumpert set a new record for speed around Germany's famous **Nürburgring** track. Many European supercar makers test their cars at "The Ring", and being fastest around it is a big deal. The Arrow is more powerful than the Gumpert, so it may grab the record back.

'Arrow-like' **aerodynamics** reduce drag and improve **downforce**

Price Tag...

Only 100 Arrows are being produced, and are expected to have a list price of around £1 million. You'll get a custom car for your money though, plus satnav and air conditioning.

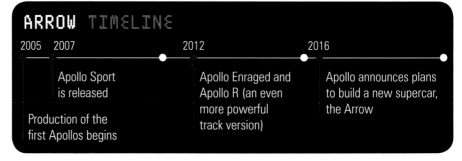

ARROW TIMELINE

2005	2007	2012	2016
	Apollo Sport is released	Apollo Enraged and Apollo R (an even more powerful track version)	Apollo announces plans to build a new supercar, the Arrow
Production of the first Apollos begins			

Chromoly steel tube frame with integral carbon **monocoque** offers maximum driver protection

Air box on roof channels air to engine, increasing power

Huge spoiler gives massive grip to rear tyres

TOP SPEED	**360** kph (223 mph)
0–100 KPH	**2.9** seconds
MAX POWER	**735** kW (986 bhp) @ 6,750 rpm
MAX TORQUE	**1000** Nm (738 lb/ft) @ 3,650 rpm

Max RPM:	not known
Engine:	3993 cc V8 twin-turbo
Weight:	1,300 kg
Fuel use per 100 km:	12.5 litres
CO2:	not known
Gearbox:	7-speed twin clutch
Drive:	all 4 wheels
Main body:	carbon fibre/aluminium
Frame:	steel/carbon/Kevlar®
Braking:	carbon-ceramic

NAME: Roland Gumpert
LIVED: 1944–present
FAMOUS AS: Founder of Apollo supercar company

Gumpert originally worked as an engineer for Audi. During the 1970s he helped create the VW (Audi) Iltis* – a military jeep. The Iltis's all-wheel drive system was developed for Audi's famous Quattro road cars. In 2004 Gumpert left Audi to start his own supercar business, called Gumpert, which used Audi engines. In 2016, the company changed its name to Apollo, and later that year Roland Gumpert left the business.

*Iltis is German for 'polecat'.

R8 V10 QUATTRO PLUS

When the R8 was released in 2006, it was a poke in the eye for the world's supercar manufacturers. Audi's first supercar was immediately voted the best in the world.

Factory: Neckarsulm, Baden-Württemberg, Germany

In 2015 the original R8 was replaced by an almost completely new version. It has a bigger engine and is more powerful. Audi owns the Italian supercar manufacturer Lamborghini. Some of the technology for the R8 comes from the Lamborghini Huracán – including the turbo-charged V10 engine.

Despite using the same engine, the Quattro Plus is very different from a Huracán. It is easy to drive, for a start. The Quattro Plus has room for a tiny bit of luggage. It can also be driven over speed bumps without getting stuck!

In 2016, an open-topped R8 Spyder was released. At the touch of a button, the Spyder's roof folds itself up and disappears. The Spyder is slightly heavier and slower than the **coupé**, but a lot more glamorous.

The V10 engine shared by the R8 and Lamborghini Huracán.

The 5.2-litre engine delivers 601 bhp through all four wheels

Fixed carbon-fibre rear wing only appears on the V10 Quattro Plus

First Audi R8, with a V8 engine and other borrowed technology from the Lamborghini Gallardo, is released

Open-topped R8 Spyder is released

Almost completely new R8, now based on the Lamborghini Huracán, comes out

(205 mph)

0–100 KPH

3.2 seconds

MAX POWER

449 kW

(601 bhp) @ 8,250 rpm

MAX TORQUE

560 Nm

(413 lb/ft) @ 6,500 rpm

NAME: August Horch
LIVED: 1868–1951
FAMOUS AS: Founder of Audi

Horch worked for Karl Benz, the founder of Mercedes Benz, before he began his own car company. *Horch* means 'listen' in German. Audi got its name because Horch's old business partners took him to court to stop him using his own name for the company. So instead, he used the Latin for 'listen' – *audi*.

What's it like to drive?

Like a dream. Like a far out, freaky, fast-forward-engaged, too many e-numbers dream [of] howling madness and gorgeous g-forces. In other words, it's pretty fast.

– carmagazine.co.uk review

Carbon-fibre mirrors, side blades and diffuser, making it 40 kg lighter than the basic R8

Laser headlights reach twice as far as normal **LED** lights

Price Tag...

It will cost you around £120,000 for the basic R8, more for the open-topped Spyder version. The R8 V10 Plus, which is the fastest R8, costs from around £134,520.

Max RPM:
8,500

Engine:
5204 cc V10

Weight:
1,630 kg

Fuel use per 100 km:
12.3 litres

CO2:
287 g/km

Gearbox:
7-speed dual-clutch automatic

Drive:
all 4 wheels

Main body:
aluminium

Frame:
aluminium-carbon monocoque

Braking:
carbon-ceramic

TT RS

Audi's RS cars are high performance versions of its normal cars. The TT RS is fitted with a souped-up **inline 5** engine – plus a whole lot of other go-faster features.

The inline 5 engine is famous among Audi lovers. An engine like this was first used in the Audi Quattro in 1980. The Quattro, as it was known, was the car to beat in **WRC**. It was famous for the unique noise of its engine. When the first TT RS appeared in 2009, Audi fans rejoiced to see that the inline 5 was back.

In 2016, a new TT RS was released. It was lighter and more powerful than the original. The power of the lightweight aluminium engine was controlled by a highly developed computer system. This made the TT RS scarily fast, but also drivable.

Large fixed rear spoiler

Suspension can be changed by the RS's computers in milliseconds, adapting to how and where the car is being driven

Double-pipe exhaust system maximises the noise of the famous 5-cylinder engine

NAME: Michèle Mouton
LIVED: 1951–present
FAMOUS AS: Groundbreaking rally driver

Michèle Mouton is one of only a few female drivers who have made it to the top in rallying. She started as a co-driver, but soon became a driver. In 1981, driving an Audi Quattro, she won the Rally San Remo and became the first woman to win a WRC rally. In 1982, Mouton won three more rallies for Audi, and finished second to Walter Röhrl (see page 25) in the World Championship.

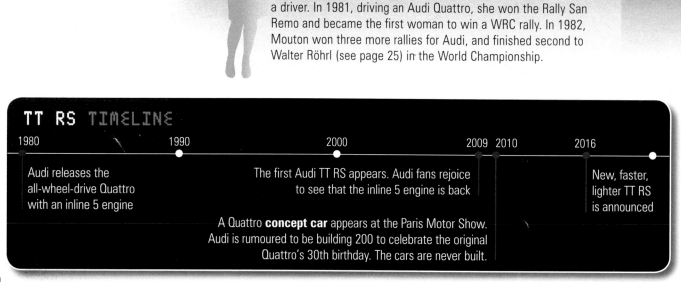

TT RS TIMELINE

1980	1990	2000	2009	2010	2016

1980 — Audi releases the all-wheel-drive Quattro with an inline 5 engine

The first Audi TT RS appears. Audi fans rejoice to see that the inline 5 engine is back

A Quattro **concept car** appears at the Paris Motor Show. Audi is rumoured to be building 200 to celebrate the original Quattro's 30th birthday. The cars are never built.

New, faster, lighter TT RS is announced

If a sports exhaust is fitted, the driver can push a dashboard button to control the noise

Tab 9

The coupé version starts at around £60,000, the Roadster a little more. So, it costs 45 per cent of the price of an R8 (see pages 8–9) and is half a second slower to reach 100 kph. Good value!

(155 mph)

0–100 KPH

3.7 seconds

MAX POWER

294 kW

(394 bhp) @ 5,850 rpm

MAX TORQUE

480 Nm

(345lb/ft) @1,700 rpm

IN • TT 3200

Large front air intakes help cool the powerful engine

Max RPM:
7,000

Engine:
2500 cc
turbo-charged inline 5

Weight:
1,440 kg

Fuel use per 100 km:
9 litres

CO2:
200 g/km

Gearbox:
7-speed dual-clutch automatic

Drive:
all 4 wheels

Main body:
aluminium and steel (est.)

Frame:
aluminium

Braking:
aluminium (optional carbon-ceramic front brakes)

What's it like to drive?

That first surge of acceleration will leave you in no doubt as to how stunningly fast the little coupé is. The power feels totally contained, however, with the Quattro deploying every ounce of the 394 bhp. It's bursting with energy...

– *www.evo.co.uk* review

IN • TT 3201

THE TT RS ROADSTER

Audi also makes a convertible version of the TT RS, known as the Roadster. This car takes 0.2 seconds longer to reach 100 kph. The convertible roof is electronically controlled and it can be lowered or raised when the car is moving. Not at top speed, though: you have to be driving at less than 50 kph.

Factory: Leipzig, Saxony, Germay

Fans of **Formula E** will recognise this BMW straight away – the i8 is used as a **safety car** during races. Whenever there is a problem on the track, the i8 zooms out and the race cars form a queue behind it.

The i8 is an unusual supercar, because it is a petrol-electric **hybrid**. A few other supercars (the McLaren P1 and the Ferrari LaFerrari) are also hybrids, but those rely mainly on a huge, powerful petrol engine, only using their electric motors for an extra boost of power when needed. The i8 is different. It has a tiny, 1.5-litre engine – the same as is used in a Mini. The rest of its power comes from electric motors.

The i8 is less powerful than other supercars, and carries a heavy electric battery. This means the rest of the car has to be super light. Many parts are made of lightweight carbon fibre, to reduce weight as much as possible.

Classic gull-wing supercar design

In Sport mode, the noise of the petrol engine is sent to speakers in the cabin, as a way of making the car sound more exciting

What's it like to drive?

Flooring the throttle gives you a smooth and muscular surge of acceleration, accompanied by a sci-fi whine from the electric motor and a deep, throaty growl from the three-cylinder engine.

– Review from *autoexpress.co.uk*

Price Tag...

It will cost you around £115,000 to buy a new i8. This is not one of the supercars that are worth more after you have bought it, though: used i8s start at about £75,000.

i8 TIMELINE

In the back are two cramped passenger seats, making the i8 one of only a few supercars that can carry more than one passenger

In 2012, BMW showed the world an open-topped i8 Concept Spyder. The car won several awards, but is not yet on sale.

Low, wide body minimises air turbulence

Weight is distributed evenly over the **axles**

TOP SPEED
250 kph
(155 mph)

0–100 KPH
4.4 seconds

MAX POWER
266 kW
(357 bhp)

MAX TORQUE
570 Nm
(420lb/ft) @ 3,700 rpm

Max RPM:
5,800

Engine:
1500 cc
3-cylinder petrol/ hybrid electric

Weight:
1,485 kg

Fuel use per 100 km:
2 litres

CO2:
49 g/km

Gearbox:
6-speed automatic

Drive:
all 4 wheels

Main body:
carbon fibre

Frame:
carbon fibre

Braking:
carbon-ceramic

THE i8S

There are rumours that BMW has been developing a lighter, more powerful version of the i8, called the i8S. Only 100 are planned. The i8S was first designed to celebrate BMW's 100th birthday, in 2016.

It is not only said to be more powerful and lighter, but it will also have better suspension, brakes and aerodynamics. Overall, these changes would mean the car could reach 100 kph in under 4 seconds.

BMW
M6 COUPÉ COMPETITION

The M6 Coupé Competition is built for speed and luxury. The suspension has a 'comfort' setting, there is space for three passengers and it even has a boot that will carry luggage! All that … and it STILL reaches 100 kph 2.4 seconds faster than a Porsche Panamera.

Factory: Dingolfing, Bavaria, Germany

The Coupé Competition is based on a standard M6, with more power. The M6 is a 'Grand Tourer', designed to drive – very quickly, but comfortably – over long distances. The Competition has a V8 engine, and is fitted with suspension and other features to help the driver handle the extra speed.

Price Tag…

Handing over about £110,000 will mean you (with the help of a rich relative) can drive away in a new M6 Competition.

Drivers can choose to change gear themselves using 'paddles' behind the steering wheel, or let the car's computer decide when to change

Large air intakes channel air to the engine and brakes for cooling, and aid aerodynamics

---

M6 COUPÉ COMPETITION TIMELINE

1983		2005	2012	2016

BMW releases the first M6, made by putting a 3500 cc engine from their disastrous M1 supercar into a 6-series grand tourer

A completely new M6, fitted with a 'power button' on the steering wheel that allowed you to switch from 400 bhp to 500 bhp

The M6 Competition is released

Another new M6, fitted with a 560 bhp V8 engine and a carbon-fibre roof; a heavier convertible version is also available

BMW Night vision screen identifies people and large animals in total darkness.

250 kph*
(155 mph)

0–100 KPH
under 4 seconds

MAX POWER
441 kW
(591 bhp) @ 6,000 rpm

MAX TORQUE
680 Nm
(501 lb/ft) @ 1,500 rpm

What's it like to drive?

The most fantastic blend of luxury and performance I've driven... Stick it in Sports mode and be rewarded with superb handling and an engine that knocks out a growl, then a thump as you change gear... Or you can switch it into Comfort, brush the sand from your hair and drive along [calmly].

– www.independent.co.uk review

Carbon-fibre roof makes the car lighter

Lightweight alloy wheels

Max RPM:
7,000

Engine:
4395 cc V8 twin-turbo

Weight:
1,925 kg

Fuel use per 100 km:
10 litres

CO2:
231 g/km

Gearbox:
7-speed dual-clutch automatic

Drive:
rear wheels

Main body:
carbon fibre

Braking:
carbon-ceramic

The Coupé Competition has three driver modes: Comfort, Sport and Sport+. These can be used to control the suspension, steering and engine power:

• In Comfort setting, the suspension is softest (best for uneven road surfaces), the steering is effortless, and the engine responds slightly less crazily.

• At the other end of the scale, in Sport+, the suspension is stiff, steering requires more effort, and the car accelerates very, very quickly. This mode is best for smooth, fast roads and **track days**.

*Can be boosted to 304 kph (189 mph) with M Driver pack

MERCEDES-AMG
GT-S

Whenever you see the letters AMG on a car, you know it will be special. AMG specialises in taking any Mercedes that is already fast … and making it even faster.

Factory: Affalterbach, Baden-Württemberg, Germany

AMG turns sports cars into supercars by making all kinds of changes. They modify the suspension, aerodynamics and interior, for example. But AMG is most famous for its engines. Each engine is built by a single worker, and every AMG engine is engraved with the signature of the worker who built it. AMG engines are not only used by Mercedes, for example, they are also fitted in the Pagani Zonda supercar.

Gear shifts can be fully automatic, or controlled by the driver using steering-wheel paddles

Drive mode can be set to Comfort (which is quietest, softest, best for long distances), Sport, Sport+ or Race (hardest, loudest and best for the racetrack)

Rear spoiler can be raised to increase downforce

Exhaust noise can be controlled by the driver, who can open or close flaps in the exhaust to change the noise

Front-mid-mounted engine (behind the front axle but in front of the driver) helps share weight almost equally between all four wheels

What's it like to drive?

This is a modern-day muscle car. It's Merc's Mustang. You sense this when you drive it... It feels raw. Much more raw than any other Mercedes and any of the other cars that you can buy for this sort of money. It feels … extremely exciting.

– Jeremy Clarkson review at *www.driving.co.uk*

Engine fitted with an ECO **stop-start system**

AMG GT-S TIMELINE

1995   2008   2015

AMG begin to release high-performance versions of the latest Mercedes SL 2-seaters

The AMG GT-S is released

SL 73 AMG, the most powerful SL model yet made; this car used the same engine as a Pagani Zonda. Only 85 SL 73s were ever made, and they are now very rare.

An AMG GT-S being used as the safety car at the Malaysia Grand Prix.

TOP SPEED

310 kph
(193 mph)

0–100 KPH

3.8 seconds

MAX POWER

375 kW
(503 bhp) @ 6,250 rpm

MAX TORQUE

650 Nm
(479 lb/ft) @ 4,750 rpm

The GT-S is a tuned-up version of the AMG-Mercedes GT – a very fast 'Grand Touring' car. The GT-S has more power, and the driver can adjust the engine, suspension and steering settings to make it perform better on a racetrack. Even so, the GT-S is still comfortable enough to drive on city streets or across the country. It even has room for your gym kit.

Max RPM:
7,000

Engine:
3982 cc V8 twin-turbo

Weight:
1,570 kg

Fuel use per 100 km:
9.6 litres

CO_2:
224 g/km

Gearbox:
7-speed dual-clutch automatic

Drive:

rear wheels

Main body:

aluminium

Frame:

aluminium **composite**

Braking:

carbon-ceramic

Price Tag...

The AMG GT-S starts at about £125,000. If you have not got quite that much, the less powerful, less racy AMG GT starts at about £105,000. But why would you want a less powerful, less racy version? Keep saving!

MERCEDES-AMG
SLS

When the SLS came out in 2010, Mercedes fans got very excited. Its design was based on one of the most famous Mercedes ever: the 300 SL Gullwing.

The Mercedes 300 SL was the design inspiration for the SLS.

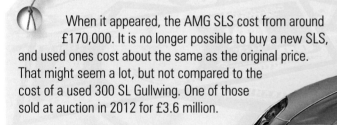

Price Tag...

When it appeared, the AMG SLS cost from around £170,000. It is no longer possible to buy a new SLS, and used ones cost about the same as the original price. That might seem a lot, but not compared to the cost of a used 300 SL Gullwing. One of those sold at auction in 2012 for £3.6 million.

SUPERCAR CONTENDER

The first supercar is usually said to be the Lamborghini Miura – but the Gullwing is another contender. It was a road-going version of the car that won the 1952 Le Mans 24-hour race. Mercedes called it a "race car for the road".

AMG SLS TIMELINE

1953		2009	2014

Mercedes create the 300 SL from their Le Mans-winning race car. Elements of its V12 engine are taken from a Second World War fighter plane, the Messerschmitt 109E.

The AMG SLS is released, featuring a similar gullwing design but with a V8 engine

AMG ends production of the SLS with the GT Final Edition – supercar fans everywhere weep

What's it like to drive?

I don't get the sense that the machine is doing all the hard work for me (although it probably is) … I'm fighting against the onslaught on understeer, balancing the car against roll in the turns, trying to find the sweet spot for the next gear change… And it feels … right.

– www.topgear.com review

NAME: Hermann Lang
LIVED: 1909–87
FAMOUS AS: Mercedes test and racing driver

Lang was originally a motorbike racer, who started working for Mercedes as a mechanic in 1927. The company realised he was a phenomenal driver, and by 1935 Lang was one of their racers. He won many races, including the Grand Prix of Tripoli three times.

Rear spoiler automatically lifts when the car reaches 120 kph

Door handles pop out when the car is unlocked, then go back in as it is driven away

Square cabin and door design similar to the 300 SL

TODAY'S SLS

The SLS, like the original Gullwing, is a race car for the road. It was developed with the help of former Formula 1 driver David Coulthard. Multiple F1 World Champion Lewis Hamilton has one, and the SLS is also a favourite with celebrities, including Floyd Mayweather Jr.

The ultimate AMG SLS is the GT Final Edition. This car has a black carbon-fibre front splitter, bonnet and fixed rear spoiler, plus black wheels. Only 350 Final Editions were made.

TOP SPEED

320 kph
(199 mph)

0–100 KPH

3.7 seconds

MAX POWER

435 kW
(583 bhp) @ 6,800 rpm

MAX TORQUE

650 Nm
(479 lb/ft) @ 4,750 rpm

Max RPM:
7,200

Engine:
6208 cc V8

Weight:
1,620 kg

Fuel use per 100 km:
13.2 litres

CO2:
308 g/km

Gearbox:
7-speed dual-clutch automatic

Drive:
rear wheels

Main body:
aluminium and plastic

Frame:
aluminium

Braking:
carbon-ceramic

PORSCHE
911 GT3 RS

The 911 is probably the most famous, most dreamed-about car Porsche makes. If you ever had a poster of a Porsche on your wall, it was probably a 911. The GT3 RS is the ultimate 911.

The 911 first appeared in 1963, and ever since it has been popular with drivers who want to go extremely fast. In fact, in 2007 a 911 driver became Britain's fastest speeder when he was caught by police doing 277 kph. He was sent to prison for 10 weeks.

The 911 was originally designed as a 2+2 road car. The GT3 RS is great on the road, good – if not better – on the racetrack. This version is lighter, more powerful, faster and has better aerodynamics than any 911 before. It is, as one reviewer said, "one of the finest Porsches ever."

DOWNFORCE AT SPEED

The faster you go in a GT3 RS, the more downforce the car creates. At 300 kph, the front splitter and wheel-arch vents create 110 kg of downforce on the front wheels. At the back, the huge rear wing and other aerodynamic features add 220 kg of downforce. This is a total of 330 kg – the same as having four adult men sitting on the roof. (If they could hang on at 300 kph…)

Vents release air behind front wheel arches, lowering air pressure inside the arches and doubling downforce

Splitter draws air in below nose of car

What's it like to drive?

Mostly we were concentrating on having fun without ending our day in a wall. This we accomplished thanks to the RS's rock-steady stability, neutral handling, and otherworldly grip.

– First-drive review on *www.caranddriver.com*

GT3 RS TIMELINE

1959	1963	1998	2015
Ferdinand Porsche draws the first designs for the 911	The first 911s go on sale in Germany: has a flat-6, air-cooled engine which, like the VW Beetle, is mounted at the back	The first liquid-cooled 911s go on sale – Porsche fans everywhere shed a tear because the traditional air-cooled engine sound has gone	The Porsche GT3 RS is released

In theory, a 911 GT3 RS will cost you a minimum of £145,000 — but there is a long waiting list. In 2015, a UK dealer advertised a used car that had been driven 227 km for £325,000. The price was so high, he said, because, "this is a car you can actually drive away today".

Larger, 53-cm rear wheels mean the GT3 RS's nose is tilted slightly downward

Gearbox changes gear automatically in 95 milliseconds (0.0095 seconds)

The GT3 RS has rear-wheel steering (the front wheels also steer, of course). It is the first Porsche to have this system.

(193 mph)

0–100 KPH

3.3 seconds

MAX POWER

368 kW

(493 bhp) @ 8,250 rpm

MAX TORQUE

460 Nm

(339 lb/ft) @ 6,250 rpm

Max RPM:
8,800

Engine:
3996 CC flat-6

Weight:
1,495 kg

Fuel use per 100 km:
12.7 litres

CO2:
296 g/km

Gearbox:
7-speed dual-clutch automatic

Drive:
rear wheels

Main body:
carbon fibre and **magnesium** alloy

Frame:
aluminium

Braking:
carbon-ceramic

NAME: Ferdinand Porsche
LIVED: 1875–1951
FAMOUS AS: Car designer

Ferdinand Porsche worked for Daimler and Mercedes-Benz, and in 1934 he designed the Volkswagen Beetle. After the Second World War, Volkswagen agreed to make him a small payment for every Beetle they sold. As over 20 million of Porsche's Beetles were eventually sold, this worked out well.

In 1959, Porsche's grandson, whose name was also Ferdinand, drew the first designs for a car that would be even more famous than the Beetle: the 911.

9FF GT9

Porsches are generally known to be pretty fast already – but they can be faster! In Dortmund, a company called 9ff turns standard Porsches into street-legal race cars. The GT9 is their fastest car.

The GT9 is based on a Porsche 911. 9ff makes several different versions of the GT9, depending on what the buyer wants the car to do*. The fastest version, the Vmax, was one of the first road cars ever to go more than 400 kph. It was recorded travelling at 437 kph. Another version, the Amax, is designed for maximum acceleration. It reaches 300 kph in fewer than 13 seconds – about as long as a Ford Fiesta takes to reach 100 kph.

A RARE SUPERCAR

Only 20 of the original GT9 Vmax cars were ever made, and no two GT9s are exactly the same. Each buyer chooses their own trim for the inside, and could have satnav, a stereo, air conditioning and other optional extras fitted.

Price Tag...

You can't buy one, at least not new: they were all sold very quickly. The price of a new GT9 Vmax was €895,000 (£797,000). For a car faster than a Bugatti Veyron, this seems cheap. On the other hand, for a car without air conditioning, satnav or even a stereo, it seems quite a lot.

Twin-turbo engine mounted in the middle of the car

Carbon-fibre body panels, doors, etc. reduce weight by almost 300 kg

Engine air intake is gold plated, to make sure air going in is as cool as possible

GT9 TIMELINE

1963
Porsche produces its first 911

2001
9ff is founded by Jan Fatthauer. His aim is to make higher-performance versions of high-performance Porsches.

2007

2008
GT9-R, a more powerful version, is released

GT9, based on a Porsche 911, is released

*The data here is for the standard version.

The GT9 is one of the world's fastest cars — faster even than a Bugatti Veyron.

364 kph
(226 mph)

0–100 KPH
3.6 seconds

MAX POWER
551 kW
(740 bhp) @ 6,800 rpm

MAX TORQUE
910 Nm
(671 lb/ft) @ 2,950 rpm

Custom-made frame with built-in roll cage and door bars for protection

Max RPM:
7,400

Engine:
3996 cc   flat-6 twin-turbo

Weight:
1,070 kg

Fuel use per 100 km:
not known

CO2:
not known

Gearbox:
6-speed **manual**

Drive:
not known

Main body:
carbon fibre

Frame:
carbon fibre

Braking:
carbon-ceramic

What's it like to drive?

When you press the throttle … it feels as though a large sumo wrestler has appeared from nowhere and sat on your chest. The engine sound is deafening. You could scream for help and no one would hear you… Just as the sumo wrestler has stood up, the twin turbos burst into action at 2500 revs and he sits back down again. At this point the scenery outside starts rushing backwards and you can almost see the bow wave of air in front.

– One of the best car reviews ever, on *www.germancarforum.com*

918 SPYDER WEISSACH

In 2013, a Porsche 918 Spyder set off around the famous Nürburgring racetrack. Six minutes and 57 seconds later, it crossed the finish line. It had smashed the record for the fastest lap by a road car.

Factory: Stuttgart, Baden-Württemberg, Germany

The car that broke the Nürburgring record was not just any Porsche Spyder – it was a Weissach edition. Compared to the original car, the Weissach is lighter and faster, with improved aerodynamics. The Weissach looks super-cool too, with a paint job that is a reminder of the racing Porsches of the 1970s.

Roof, rear spoiler, mirrors and windscreen surround are all carbon fibre, reducing weight

PETROL-ELECTRIC POWER

Like every 918 Spyder, the Weissach is a hybrid-power car; running off petrol and electricity. For petrol power it has a snorting **normally aspirated** V8 engine. It gets an extra boost of power from two electric motors, one for each axle. The electric battery can be fully charged in fewer than 30 minutes.

The Spyder's exhaust pipes point up from the engine. One test driver described them as sounding, "like the arrival of a swarm of very angry mutant horror wasps, played through AC-DC's sound system."

Price Tag...

It will cost you in the region of £800,000, before you start adding extras such as a stereo or air conditioning.

918 SPYDER WEISSACH TIMELINE

2004
Porsche releases the Carrera GT, like the 918 a mid-engined supercar. It is powered by a V10 petrol engine.

2013
The first 918 Spyder petrol-electric hybrid goes on sale

2015
After 918 cars have been sold, production of the 918 Spyder ends

What's it like to drive?

I turned the knob to Sport Hybrid mode and heard the sonic boom. And then I went for the full-fat Race Hybrid setting and it felt as though I were slingshotting round the moon.

– Jeremy Clarkson on *www.driving.co.uk*.

Carbon blades improve aerodynamics

Magnesium wheels reduce weight by 15 kg

NAME: Walter Röhrl
LIVED: 1947–present
FAMOUS AS: Race and rally driver; Porsche test driver

One of the world's best ever rally drivers, Röhrl was once described by Niki Lauda as a "genius on wheels". Coming from a three-times Formula 1 World Champion, this comment really means something.
After retiring from racing Röhrl became a test driver for Porsche. He is now their chief test driver, and has helped develop many of Porsche's most famous supercars.

TOP SPEED
345 kph
(160 mph)

0–100 KPH
2.6 seconds

MAX POWER
652 kW
(874 bhp) @ 8,500 rpm

MAX TORQUE
1280 Nm
(944 lb/ft) @ 6,700 rpm

Max RPM:
9,150

Engine:
4593 cc V8 plus two electric motors

Weight:
1,634 kg

Fuel use per 100 km:
3.0 litres

CO2:
70 g/km

Gearbox:
7-speed dual-clutch automatic

Drive:
all 4 wheels

Main body:
carbon fibre

Frame:
carbon fibre

Braking:
carbon-ceramic

PORSCHE
718 BOXSTER S

Factory: Stuttgart, Baden-Württemberg, Germany

Most Porsche supercars have the engine at the back. The Boxster is different: it is **rear-mid engined**. Many drivers feel that this makes the Boxster one of the best-handling Porsches you can get.

Having the engine further forward shares its weight more equally between all four wheels. More weight on the wheels gives the tyres more grip. This makes the Boxster great fun to drive fast on a bendy road.

The 718 Boxster S features a turbo-charged **flat-4** engine – different from the flat-6 which powers most Porsches. To begin with fans were outraged, but fortunately the Boxster S turned out to be completely brilliant to drive.

The Porsche 718 S has an **ergonomic**, sporty interior, with a choice of finishes.

What's it like to drive?

You put your foot down and feel your internal organs [being] squeezed to one side under the sheer g-force … it can throw you at the horizon with sufficient force to make you feel physically uncomfortable.

– review by *autocar.co.uk*

BOXSTER S TIMELINE

1957	1969		2010	2016

The 914 is released: a mid-engined, targa-topped sports car

The Boxster Spyder is released

The 718 Spyder race car appears. Many of its design features (for example, the speed hump behind the seat) are also seen on the modern 718 Spyder

Boxster S, with a new flat-4 turbo-charged engine instead of a traditional Porsche flat-6

Note: data is for an automatic car with Sport Chrono extras.

Optional 'launch' control button: drivers push this when they want to do the fastest possible start

'Comfort' and 'sport' mode selector: sport is aimed at race tracks and smooth, fast roads

Roll bars behind seats are made of mixed steel and aluminium

Roll bar for windscreen is made of steel

(177 mph)

0–100 KPH

4.2 seconds

MAX POWER

257 kW

(345 bhp) @ 6,500 rpm

MAX TORQUE

420 Nm

(310 lb/ft) @ 1,900 rpm

 Max RPM:
7,400

 Engine:
2497 cc $^{\text{flat-4 turbo}}$

 Weight:
1,385 kg

 Fuel use per 100 km:
7.3 litres

 CO2:
167 g/km

 Gearbox:
6-speed manual or
7-speed dual-clutch automatic

 Drive:
rear wheels

Main body:
steel/aluminium

Frame:
steel/aluminium

Braking:
aluminium
(carbon-ceramic optional)

DOWN ON POWER, UP ON THRILLS

The Boxster S has less than half the power of a 918 Spyder Weissach. However, it has a stripped-out cabin (Porsche even replaced the door handles with fabric loops to reduce weight), lightweight **bucket seats** and some of the soundproofing material removed. With the optional manual gearbox, it feels like a totally modern version of an old-fashioned street-racing car.

Price Tag...

In the world of supercars, the 718 S is a bit of a bargain: it starts at about £57,000. This means for the same cost as a single 918 Weissach, you could buy eleven 718 Spyders and still have enough money left over for a dream holiday.

The supercars in this book are some of the newest, fastest and most exciting supercars made in Germany. But lots of other amazing German supercars have recently been manufactured. Here are a few of them:

MANUFACTURER: LOTEC
MODEL: C1000
YEAR: 1995

As rare as a supercar can be: only one was ever made. It was built for a wealthy oilman from the United Arab Emirates, and was said to have cost him $US 3.4 million (£2.6 million). Rumours say it reached 431 kph (268 mph), making it one of the world's fastest cars.

MANUFACTURER: MERCEDES
MODEL: CLK-GTR
YEAR: 1997

Like the Porsche 911 GT1 Strassenversion, the CLK-GTR was built as a **homologation** special. Only 25 were made: Mercedes kept the first one, so only 24 were ever sold. The race car was designed for GT1 and Le Mans 24-Hour racing, and the road version was almost identical.

MANUFACTURER: MERCEDES
MODEL: SL65 AMG BLACK SERIES
YEAR: 2008

As Mercedes said: "Limited production. Unlimited performance". The raw statistics of 100 kph in 3.8 seconds and a limited top speed of 320 kph (199 mph) show that the SL65 was a proper supercar.

MANUFACTURER: PORSCHE
MODEL: CARRERA GT
YEAR: 2004

The Carrera GT is sometimes described as one of the last supercars without lots of electronic driver aids. With a targa top, and a 612 bhp, V10-engine, only 1,270 of these were ever made.

MANUFACTURER: PORSCHE
MODEL: 911 GT1 STRASSENVERSION
YEAR: 1996

Porsche built just 25 road-going versions of this car, making it super-rare. Built to satisfy homologation rules for GT-class racing, this really is a race car you can drive on the road.

MANUFACTURER: PORSCHE
MODEL: 996 GT1
YEAR: 1996

This road-going version of Porsche's race car had a classic flat-6 engine and would hit 100 kph in 3.6 seconds. You could buy one for around £400,000, as long as you didn't expect things like interior trim or a stereo.

MANUFACTURER: MERCEDES
MODEL: SLR MCLAREN
YEAR: 2003

Before McLaren became a supercar manufacturer on its own, it worked with Mercedes. The ultimate result was the SLR. Several different versions were made, but the most wonderful to look at was the SLR Stirling Moss. This is a Batman-style version of an old open-cockpit racing car, the 1955 300 SLR (see page 30).

High-performance German cars were among the first to compete in races, in the early 1900s. Ever since, companies such as Mercedes, Porsche and BMW have been building amazing cars for people who like to drive fast and look good. Here are just a few of the most famous German supercars from the past:

MANUFACTURER: BMW
MODEL: 507
YEAR: 1956

The 507 was a bit of a disaster for BMW. It cost too much to make, which meant it ended up costing buyers twice as much as planned. Despite being popular with celebrities (Elvis Presley had one), only 252 were ever made. Today, only 202 are known to survive: each is worth over $1 million (around £800,000).

MANUFACTURER: MERCEDES BENZ
MODEL: SL300 GULLWING
YEAR: 1954

So beautiful it makes you want to cry (because you'll never own one), the Gullwing was also an extremely high-performance car. It was the world's fastest road car and a multiple race winner.

MANUFACTURER: MERCEDES BENZ
MODEL: 300 SLR
YEAR: 1955

The great British driver Stirling Moss drove a 300 SLR in the 1955 World Sportscar Championship. The championship was six races long, and Moss missed the first two. He then won three of the last four races: the **Mille Miglia**, RAC Tourist Trophy and the **Targa Florio**. Mercedes won the manufacturers' prize.

MANUFACTURER: PORSCHE
MODEL: 356
YEAR: 1948

The 356 is powered by an 1100 cc flat-4 engine, and hardly counts as a supercar. But this was the first Porsche ever and even today you can tell it's a Porsche.

MANUFACTURER: PORSCHE
MODEL: 914
YEAR: 1970

The 914 was a joint development between Porsche and Volkswagen, known as the 'VW Porsche'. The 914 was mid-engined (unlike most rear-engined Porsches), but was available with a classic flat-6 Porsche engine. To save weight, some parts of the bodywork were fibreglass.

UK

NATIONAL MOTOR MUSEUM

John Montagu Bldg
Beaulieu
Brockenhurst
Hampshire
SO42 7ZN

http://nationalmotormuseum.org.uk/
Supercars
Not a specialist supercar museum,
and focusing mainly on British cars,
the National Motor Museum is still
a great place for car fans to visit.
Its website has details of special
displays, which sometimes include
supercars.

BRITISH MOTOR MUSEUM

Banbury Road
Gaydon
Warwickshire
CV35 0BJ

https://www.britishmotormuseum.
co.uk
Like the National Motor Museum,
many of the cars are British, but other
countries' cars are also on display.

HAYNES MOTOR MUSEUM

Haynes International Motor Museum
Sparkford
Yeovil
Somerset
BA22 7LH

http://www.haynesmotormuseum.
com
With one collection known as
'Supercar Century', this is a must-visit
if you are nearby.

GERMANY

BMW MUSEUM

Am Olympiapark 1
80809 München

http://www.bmw-welt.com/en/
index.html
Not only cars, but also motorbikes
can be seen at the BMW Museum.
There is a permanent display of
over 100 vehicles from all eras of
BMW. There are also temporary
exhibitions on subjects such as
the history of BMW.

MERCEDES MUSEUM

Mercedesstrasse 100
70372 Stuttgart

https://www.mercedes-benz.com/
en/mercedes-benz/classic/museum/
This is an amazing museum for
car lovers, especially if they like
Mercedes.

Many of the most famous Mercedes
road and track cars are on display,
starting with 3-wheelers that look
more like bicycles and ending with
the company's supercars.

PORSCHE MUSEUM

Porscheplatz 1
70435 Stuttgart-Zuffenhausen

http://www.porsche.com/
museum/en/
People visit the Porsche Museum to
see the amazing architecture, as well
as the amazing cars. There are almost
100 Porsches from various times on
display, plus special exhibitions about
particular cars, events or races.

2+2 car with two main seats in the front and two small, usually uncomfortable seats behind

aerodynamics how air flows around an object

axle rod connecting the wheels on opposite sides of a car

bucket seat seat with a rounded back that fits around your sides, which holds you in place when going round a corner at high speed

composite made up of several materials

convertible car design where the roof can fold down

coupé car with a fixed, solid roof, two doors and a sloping rear

downforce downward pressure on the tyres, which makes them grip the road better

drive system providing power to the wheels, for example rear-wheel drive, front-wheel drive and all-wheel drive

ergonomic designed to maximise comfort and performance

flat-4/6 engine with four or six cylinders arranged in two horizontal rows (lying flat), with two or three cylinders in each row

Formula E series of races for electric-powered cars

homologation rules that allow a car to be entered in a particular race category. Usually a certain number of that particular car must be sold for use on the road

hybrid a type of engine that uses power from more than one source, usually in cars an internal combustion engine combined with electric motors.

inline 5 engine with five cylinders arranged all in a row

LED short for Light-Emitting Diode, a kind of bright-white light used in some car headlights

magnesium alloy metal that is lighter, stronger and better at absorbing vibration than aluminium

manual gears the driver has to change for herself, using a gearstick

mid-mounted describes an engine that is behind the driver and passenger seats, where its weight helps all four wheels grip the road

Mille Miglia translated as 'thousand miles', the Mille Miglia is a famous Italian race held on public roads between 1927 and 1957

monocoque a special vehicle frame that gets its strength from its outer layer, instead of a supporting frame (*monocoque* = single cell in French)

normally aspirated engine that is not fitted with turbo chargers

Nürburgring world-class motorsports track and facilities in Nürburg, Germany

rear-mid engine with the engine behind the driver but in front of the rear wheels

safety car car driven around in front of a line of racing cars to slow them down, if there has been an accident during a race

stop-start system computer-controlled system for stopping a car when it is not moving, then restarting it again when the driver wants to move off. Stop-start systems are a way of saving fuel and causing less pollution

street legal allowed to be driven on public roads

Targa Florio motor race held in the mountains of Sicily between 1907 and 1977

torque the amount of 'work' exerted by an engine

track day when ordinary drivers can pay to drive on a race track. Sometimes a race car and instruction from a racing driver are part of the experience

WRC short for World Rally Championship